David was a PIRATE

By
Dixie Benshoff Ludick

Illustrated By Nancy W. Gabalac

Dr. Dixie Benshoff Ludick is a psychologist with twenty years experience. She is currently working with schools in the State of Ohio seeing lots of children who are in kindergarten and who believe that they are pirates, cowboys, ballerinas, and astronauts. She lives with her husband, Tim Ludick, an attorney, and son, David, age 5, in Aurora, Ohio, and recently lost Bunker, the Golden Retriever, who passed away during this project. She and Nancy Gabalac, the illustrator, have been friends since their graduate school days. This is their first children's book.

Copyright © 2000, by Dixie L. Benshoff & Nancy W. Gabalac
All rights reserved

DEDICATED TO
DAVID,

a true pirate, who captured my heart with his Jolly Roger imagination and his unquenchable thirst for the Treasure of Knowledge. I will love you forever, my son.

Dixie Benshoff Ludick

David

was a pirate.

He just knew it!

He knew it when he put on his tattered shorts

and striped shirt.

He knew it when he put a bandana around his head.

He knew it when he strapped on his sword and tipped his tri-cornered pirate hat rakishly over one eye,

usually the eye with a black patch.

The trouble was that others did not seem to know it.

*"David, get that patch off your eye;
you'll wreck your vision!"*

*"David, don't wave that sword about;
you'll put someone's eye out!"*

"David, if you cut up one more pair of your trousers, so help me..."

All Summer long David hunted for pirate treasures.

He sailed to pirate island.

He dug for buried treasure.

He fought Spanish ships.

One day as he was making his dog, Bunker, "walk the plank",

his mom called to him-

"David, come in and change clothes. We are going to kindergarten screening."

David wasn't sure what kindergarten screening was, but he knew that if it was something he had to change clothes for, he wasn't going to like it.

"Are there pirates there?" he wanted to know.

His mother just looked at him—one hand on her hip and the other pointing to the bathroom door.

Guess what! There weren't any pirates there.

*There wasn't even anyone who said "Argh", Ahoy Matey",
or "Walk the Plank".*

All summer long

David worried about kindergarten,

but not so much that he forgot to play pirates.

Then one morning it was time to go to kindergarten.

He couldn't wear his pirate clothes, but he tucked a small piece of paper with a skull and crossbones drawn on it in his pants, just in case.

Miss Wright met him at the door.

She seemed happy to see him which he wondered about, since most people aren't happy to see pirates.

She gave him a snack of crackers and juice, which he described to the other children as "hard tack and rum".

This made him feel a little better.

Then Miss Wright taught him how to sing "Row, Row, Row Your Boat" and "My Bonnie Lies Over the Ocean" which pleased him even more.

But the best part was when Miss Wright called all the children to the carpet and began to read out loud:

The Old Sea Dog

Squire Trelawney and Dr. Livesey have asked me, Jim Hawkins, to write down the story of Treasure Island. I will tell you everything, just as it happened. The only thing I won't tell you is where the island is. That's because there is still treasure buried there.

And right then and there David just knew that he was a pirate,

and that Miss Wright knew it too.

www.ingramcontent.com/pod-product-compliance
Lightning Source LLC
Chambersburg PA
CBHW041437040426
42453CB00021B/2453